Dr. Dan Johnson

Dan Johnson is a husband, father, grandfather, and school superintendent whose study of personality and group dynamics has spanned 30 years. For the past ten years he has used Real Colors in workshops with student, teacher, parent, and business groups throughout the country.

Dr. Johnson, who now resides in Loveland, Colorado, attributes his survival as a Green-Orange to his Blue wife. And he insists that he could never have survived as a school superintendent without the help of numerous Gold staff members.

About NCTI

Since 1981, The National Curriculum & Training Institute, Inc. ("NCTI") has gained a reputation as a leader in the training industry. This reputation was earned because of our unique history focused on understanding human behavior. This insight into human behavior provides us with the expertise to design and deliver successful training programs such as the one you recently attended on Real Colors®.

NCTI's highly skilled and experienced trainers have traveled throughout the globe working with correctional and educational agencies, government agencies, businesses, and professional organizations to assist them in areas such as the following:

- Motivating their workforce
- Communicating more effectively
- Developing inter-personal relationships
- Dealing with differing Learning, Teaching, and Leadership Styles
- Managing their human resources effectively

It is NCTI's belief that when individuals are allowed to gain insights into their own personality preference and that of others, significant skill development occurs long before the NCTI workshops are completed.

Congratulations!

Since you are reading this book, you have probably attended one of The National Curriculum & Training Institute's (NCTI) Real Colors® workshops or have had a similar introductory experience with temperament. If so, you know that temperament is not a new concept. It dates back to Plato (340 B.C.) and runs through the 20th Century from Myers-Briggs (1962) to David Keirsey (1998).

Keirsey is one of the most significant contributors to the concept of temperament. His work has inspired numerous research studies and follow-up strategies in the temperament field. Therefore, while other research studies pertaining to temperament and type may be cited in this guide, NCTI's Real Colors relies primarily on Keirsey's research. Real Colors, one of the most widely used temperament tools available today, provides a hands-on practical way to think about and interact with people through a temperament lens.

Now that you have had an introduction to Real Colors, you are ready to take the next step – to gain a deeper understanding and appreciation for the colors and their use in everyday life.

We have chosen to use a homeowner's analogy for this guide to emphasize the role that the colors can play in your life. Real Colors is like a home for your personality. When you learn to apply the colors in a balanced way, you will feel safe enough to invite others into your world and, in turn, feel more relaxed in their world.

That is the purpose of this guide – to review the fundamental principles underlying Real Colors, to provide practical descriptions of the four colors, and to explore ways to use colors to gain a better understanding of your own personality as well as to improve relationships with others. We know you will find the guide useful as an ongoing reference. **For more information on Real Colors and all Real Colors products and services, you can call (800) 622-1644.**

Contents

The Basic Real Colors Floor Plan

"If a man does not keep pace with his companions,
perhaps it is because he hears a different drummer.
Let him step to the music which he hears,
however measured or far away."

–Henry D. Thoreau

Thoreau's message strikes a positive note with most people, but most of us would admit that we haven't quite figured out how to step to our own music without drowning out everyone else's song. It is difficult to strike a balance between being ourselves and getting along with the rest of the world. Real Colors alone can't guarantee this balance in your life, but it does offer a basic floor plan from which you can design your own sense of balance.

Now that you have been introduced to the colors, "What comes next?" You have a general understanding of your own strengths and liabilities and you can identify Blue, Gold, Green, and Orange in others. But how can you apply this concept in your day-to-day life experiences? In other treatments of this topic (Johnson, 2003), I have compared temperament to having a floor plan for a four-room house, as illustrated in Figure 1.1.

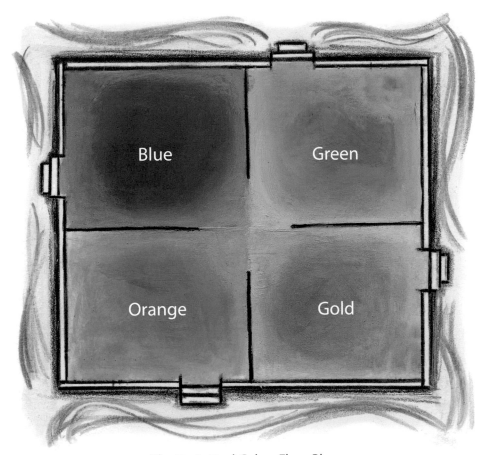

The Basic Real Colors Floor Plan
Figure 1.1

The Basic Real Colors Floor Plan

This figure represents a starting point from which you can design your own Real Colors home. The trick is to make your home safe and comfortable for yourself and at the same time inviting to others. Each room in this house has its own exterior entrance. You will tend to use one of these four entrances more than the other three, and once inside the house, you will spend more time in some rooms than in others. But you can learn to use different entrances from time to time and to feel comfortable in any room. You can also make your home more inviting to others by allowing them to enter through the door that feels most comfortable to them. As you allow yourself to flow more comfortably from room to room, you may want to consider how you can redecorate, renovate, and even expand this basic floor plan.

We all develop skills and characteristics that feel comfortable and tend to lose sight of other ways of thinking about our world. We tend to choose friends and career paths that mesh with or complement these comfort zones. Unfortunately, such preferences can limit life experiences and life options. When we become so accustomed to entering our Real Colors house through the same door and spending most of our time in one or two rooms, our experience is at best limiting and at worst self-defeating. Bobby, a fifth grader, put it this way: "A liability is nothing more than a strength we carry too far." Figure 1.2 illustrates this point.

Figure 1.2 represents a color order of Green-Orange-Blue-Gold. This person has become so accustomed to using the Green door to his Real Colors home that over the years he has made this room larger (to hold all his Green stuff). He has had positive experiences in following his color order. Parents, teachers, and friends have rewarded his attitudes and behaviors in

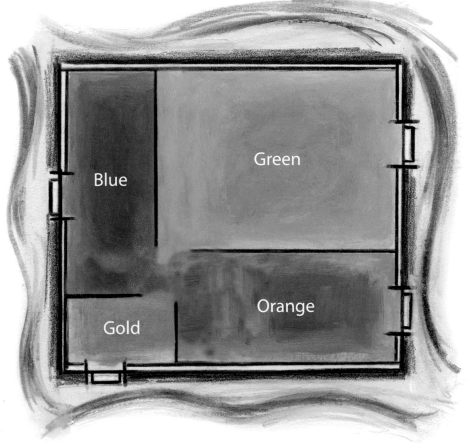

From Strength to Liability
Figure 1.2

numerous situations. But look at what has happened to the size of the Blue and Gold rooms. They are significantly smaller than the Green and Orange rooms. They are also more removed from the Green entrance most often used by this individual. Sometimes we develop a strength to such an extent that we impede other areas of our personality. We are so busy functioning in our preferred color that we forget to develop other colors. This imbalance makes it difficult to achieve the balance in our lives that we need to enjoy ourselves and the people around us.

At the same time, we have all experienced the tension of not being appreciated for who we are. Parents, family, friends, and work responsibilities often prevent us from being who we are, from spending enough time in our preferred room, or from moving from room to room in the order that feels most comfortable for us. Figure 1.3 illustrates this situation. In this figure, the individual's preferred color is still Green, but other forces have prevented the normal development of this preference. Notice what happens when an individual lacks the opportunity to develop from a position of strength.

This Green has seldom been appreciated for her preferences. Parents, teachers, and friends have discouraged her Green attitudes and behaviors in numerous situations. When she has attempted to exercise her Green-Orange tendencies, she has been told to be more organized, on time, etc. – more Gold. Her natural temperament tendencies have been overshadowed by the Gold. (Note the dotted line indicating Gold stuff overflowing into the Green, Orange, and Blue rooms.) Other people in her life have emphasized

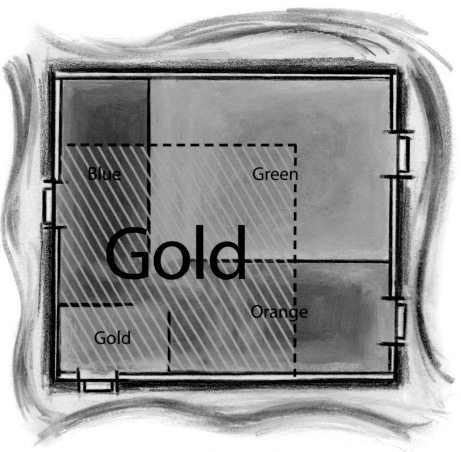

From Liability to Liability
Figure 1.3

her weakest or least comfortable color (Gold). Notice, however, that the Gold is represented as a shadow impeding on the other colors.

In most cases it is difficult, if not impossible, to change a person's color order. Moreover, it is generally counterproductive for parents, spouses, or employers to focus on a person's liabilities or least preferred color.

A negative approach generally will not get that person to achieve to a higher level of expectation in a liability area. In the process, it may even lower the person's ability to achieve in their preferred color. The moral of the story is to focus first on a person's strengths. Enter their Real Colors home through their preferred room, and they may invite your opinion about other rooms of the house.

We often experience some degree of stress when we are forced to enter our Real Colors home through doors other than our preferred door (in this situation, Green). We focus so much on our liabilities that we fail to develop our natural strengths. Although we will consider these factors in more detail later in this guide, let's take a moment to review the color balance in general.

The fundamental message of Real Colors is that the first step in getting along with others is getting along with yourself – understanding and accepting who you are. Victor Frankl (1959) described this balance as a "search for meaning." Your Real Colors presenter described it as the ability to be your own color while still doing all of the colors.

The balance between personal fulfillment and getting along with others is seldom perfect and never static. The people and events of our world affect the range and intensity of our colors. And that range and intensity is shifting constantly. It depends on the support we get in our formative years, the opportunities we have, and the consequences we face as a result of our successes or our mistakes. If we are surrounded by family and friends who support us in good times and bad, people who encourage us to build on our strengths, our success may become an avenue to develop other skills and attitudes. On the other hand, if we are constantly chided for our failures, we may simply withdraw or wait for others to tell us what to think and do.

Real Colors balance is dynamic and multifaceted. Let's take a closer look at how this makes being human both exciting and exasperating. This fundamental principle is illustrated in Figure 1.4.

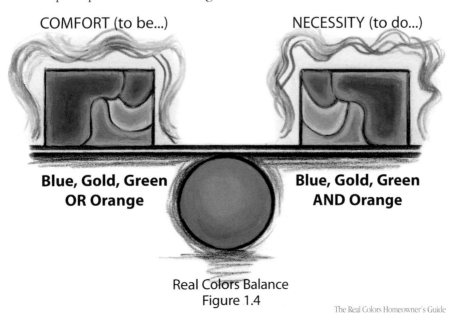

COMFORT (to be...)   NECESSITY (to do...)

Blue, Gold, Green
OR Orange

Blue, Gold, Green
AND Orange

Real Colors Balance
Figure 1.4

⑤ The Basic Real Colors Floor Plan

David Keirsey's research (1998) indicates that Oranges and Golds comprise between 80 and 90 percent of the general population – approximately 45-50 percent Gold and 35-40 percent Orange. Blues and Greens combined, comprise the other 13-17 percent with about 8-10 percent being Blue and 5-7 percent being Green.

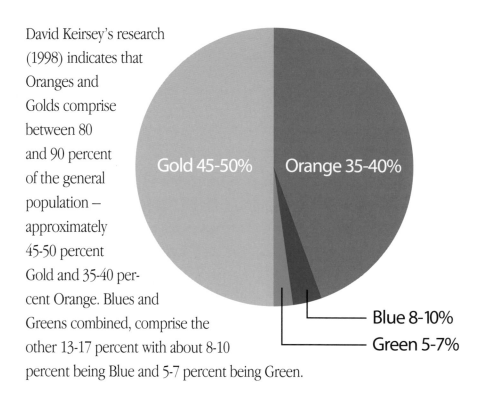

Gold 45-50%

Orange 35-40%

Blue 8-10%

Green 5-7%

(See www.keirsey.com for more current statistics.)

In general, Golds and Oranges can be said to find meaning in concrete, real-world experiences. Blues and Greens search for meaning in a more abstract world – in connections that lie beyond facts and events. While both Golds and Oranges focus initially on concrete events and experiences, they process those experiences in different ways. Likewise, Blues and Greens both focus on connections among events and experiences, but they process those connections from significantly different perspectives.

Figure 1.5 summarizes the similarities and differences among the four colors.

CONCRETE	ABSTRACT
Orange – interact with the world through the senses and try to be open to as many experiences as possible. They tend to be active and basically non-judgmental.	**Blue** – interact with the world in terms of feelings and intuition. They tend to see life in terms of spiritual connections throughout the universe.
Gold – interact through the senses according to clear standards and expectations. They tend to classify, limit, and judge information.	**Green** – interact with the world through ideas and principles. They tend to see the universe as connected through logic and reason.

Color Similarities and Differences
Figure 1.5

⑤ The Basic Real Colors Floor Plan

Concrete people, Golds and Oranges, find meaning in the daily facts and events of what we might call the "real world." They focus on the real world through their senses of sight, hearing, smell, touch, and taste. Oranges are tacticians who value facts and events as potential opportunities to discover and enjoy. Golds tend to be logistical, valuing facts and events in terms of how they fit predefined parameters.

Abstract people, Blues and Greens, find meaning in what is often referred to as the "big picture." They function more intuitively, focusing on the connections between and among people and events. Blues focus on the spiritual or emotional impact of facts and events. Greens focus on logical connections and underlying principles. Among these intuitive, big-picture folks, Blues outnumber Greens.

However, a more significant point may be the imbalance between concretes and abstracts. As previously indicated, Oranges and Golds combined compose 80-90 percent of the general population while Blues and Greens combined compose only 13-17 percent of the general population. And this minority status has both advantages and disadvantages. For example, it is obviously easier for Golds or Oranges to find people who share similar views of the world. There are simply more of them. Golds can find other Golds to reinforce their focus on order and probability. Oranges can find other Oranges to reinforce and support their interest in uniqueness and adventure. But since there are fewer Blues and Greens in the world, the abstract individuals find themselves having to fit in. On the other hand, their unique way of looking at the world can create a special demand for their abilities and services. Figure 1.6 illustrates the significance of this imbalance.

While Golds and Oranges may appreciate Blues and Greens for their unique way of seeing the world, they may only be able to appreciate them in small doses. A prime example of this can be seen in the public schools where nearly 70 percent of adults are Gold. These adult Golds can wax philosophically for hours about the need to understand differences, the need for students to be more logical (Green) or creative (Blue). Yet, when it comes to evaluating or rewarding students, teachers demonstrate their own values very clearly. Creative and independent-thinking students often find themselves staying in for recess for having failed to complete their assignments or losing points on assignments for having failed to follow directions.

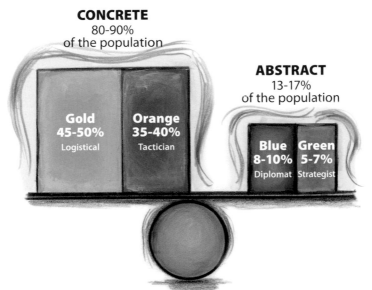

The Concrete-Abstract Imbalance
Figure 1.6

◐ The Basic Real Colors Floor Plan

At the same time, we should be very careful not to stereotype any color. Our life experiences, how we are appreciated or unappreciated for who we are, has a tremendous influence on our actions. Even when our colors sort into the same order, they may differ in intensity. Your Real Colors presenter exposed you to several activities that helped you see how your colors flow within your own Real Colors floor plan. You sorted the color cards by pictures and then by written descriptors. Then you took the color survey to get a numeric score, and later you moved to like color groups for additional activities. With each activity you gained a deeper understanding of the similarities and differences among the colors. At some point during or after those activities you may have thought, "I'm Blue, but I'm not off the deep end like some of those folks." Let's take Joe as an example.

Joe's personality rainbow during the Real Colors workshop was Green, Gold, Orange, Blue. Given that his first color is Green, Joe tends to focus on the world in abstract rather than concrete terms. Joe's first concrete color is Gold. So we can refer to him as a Green-Gold.

But what does this tell us about Joe? In other words, what makes Joe as a Green-Gold different from Bob, who is a Green-Orange?

Joe's first color (Green) tells us that he likes to interact with his world in terms of abstract principles. As a Green, Joe tends to focus on connections in terms of underlying ideas and principles. But as a Green-Gold, Joe tends to focus his abstract reasoning on what already exists (Gold) rather than on what could be (Orange). Let's look at this concrete-abstract combination in a bit more detail.

As you read the following descriptions, start with the one that describes you to see how comfortable it feels. Then move to the other descriptions. (Greens, please don't spend too much time over-analyzing these scenarios.) As you consider who you are according to the colors, first identify your strongest tendency. Is your preferred color concrete or abstract? If it is abstract, identify your strongest concrete color next (and vice versa). You can use this abstract-concrete or concrete-abstract combination to gain a broader perspective of who you are across the color continuum. We'll focus heavily on these color combinations as we proceed through the guide.

Abstracts – Blues and Greens

Blue-Gold vs. Blue-Orange

With Blue as their first color, Blue-Golds focus on abstract spiritual or emotional connections. But the Gold (follow-up color) applies that focus to emotional connections within certain learned and clearly defined parameters. If a Blue-Gold has to choose between human needs and rules, they will typically fall on the side of people. At the same time, Blue-Golds like to deal with human needs in terms of "reasonable and predictable" parameters. Blue-Oranges, on the other hand, are more likely to accept or even to pursue people who are unique and unpredictable.

*Examples: Blue-Golds might be effective social workers who meet clients'
needs within the available resources of the system. Blue-Oranges might be
effective social workers who feel compelled to step outside the system to meet
clients' unique needs with less regard for cost or protocol. Blue-Golds want
people to have meaningful experiences. Blue-Oranges find meaning in most
experiences.*

Green-Gold vs. Green-Orange

Green-Golds focus on logical connections among ideas and principles. If a
Green-Gold needs to choose between abstract principles and specific laws
or parameters, they will choose abstract principles. However, Green-Golds
prefer to deal with ideas that improve existing structures in incremental,
measurable ways. They are often leery of ideas that are unproven or experi-
mental. Green-Oranges, on the other hand, are more likely to apply abstract
principles in unique ways. They like to invent something new. Green-
Oranges are less predictable than Green-Golds and much more likely to
accept mistakes as a normal part of problem solving.

*Examples: Green-Gold scientists might be effective civil engineers applying
their logical problem solving to create strong, functional bridges. They will
develop plans based on accepted engineering theories and practices. Green-
Orange scientists might be effective architects who create new bridge models
outside the accepted scientific principles of the day. Green-Golds search for a
better way to do something. Green-Oranges search for something better to do.*

Concretes – Golds and Oranges

Gold-Blue vs. Gold-Green

With Gold as their first color, Gold-Blues focus on concrete, real-life experiences. The Blue (follow-up color) causes them to process those concrete events in terms of their emotional connections to other people and events in their lives. Gold-Blues use past experiences to sort or judge people and events in terms of their fit with accepted parameters. If Gold-Blues have to choose between people who follow rules or people who take chances, they will generally fall on the side of rules. Gold-Greens, on the other hand, tend to focus more on the logical connections among events, seeming at times to ignore the people altogether. Gold-Greens want rules that make logical sense, while Gold-Blues might prefer rules that make people happy.

> *Examples: Gold-Blues might be effective teachers who focus on rules and procedures as a way of meeting their students' needs. Gold-Greens might be effective teachers who focus on rules and procedures as a way of preparing their students for the next grade level. Gold-Blues are interested in quality people. Gold-Greens find quality in interesting people.*

Orange-Blue vs. Orange-Green

Oranges are interested in immediacy. They want to experience real people and events now. Orange-Blues tend to choose activities that involve them with other people, often in competitive situations. To Orange-Blues, competition is a form of bonding. Orange-Greens, on the other hand, are often more interested in the score than in whether or not other people are having fun. Orange-Greens may even choose more solitary activities where they compete with themselves.

> *Examples: Orange-Blues might be effective salespeople who believe their product will make customers' lives more exciting and productive. Orange-Greens might be effective salespeople who believe customers will understand that their product is the best on the market. Orange-Blues seek unique experiences that impress people. Orange-Greens seek experiences that impress unique people.*

It is impossible to separate feelings from cognition, senses from intuition. It is also impossible to know whether our genetic make-up or our life experiences have more impact on our temperament. What we do know is that we are all capable of employing the tactics of the Orange, the logistics of the Gold, the diplomacy of the Blue, and the strategies of the Green. The extent to which we do so probably depends on both genetics and experience.

Bill, who could best be described as a Green-Gold, is a good example of this nature-nurture balance. Bill was a Korean orphan raised by a U.S. family from the age of three. His natural rainbow is Green, Gold, Orange, Blue. His adoptive parents are Green, Orange, Blue, Gold and Blue, Orange, Green, Gold. Despite Bill's parents' admonitions to "loosen-up," Bill would never put his Gold far enough behind to take significant risks. At the same time, his parents' admonitions certainly made Bill less rigid than he might have been if raised by parents who simply reinforced his Green-Gold tendencies.

The trick is to learn to appreciate who we are and understand how we relate to others. In the next chapter, we will consider how various obstacles impede our movement from room to room within the basic Real Colors floor plan. But first, take a moment to reflect on the following questions as a way of thinking about your own Real Colors balance.

1. What is the order of your color rainbow? _____

_____

Given your Real Colors workshop experience and what you have read in this chapter, draw the four rooms of your Real Colors floor plan in the box below (largest room for most preferred color to smallest room for least preferred color).

2. How does your floor plan compare to people around you – parents, spouse, friends, etc.?_____

_____

_____

_____

3. How comfortable are you with your floor plan? _____

_____

_____

_____

4. How effective are you at making others feel comfortable within your floor plan?

_____

_____

_____

_____

_____

_____

5. How comfortable are you within other people's floor plans? _____

_____

_____

_____

_____

Interior Design in Your Real Colors Home

Interior Design in Your Real Colors Home

"[Flow is] the state in which people are so involved in an activity that nothing else seems to matter; the experience itself is so enjoyable that people will do it even at great cost, for the sheer sake of doing it."

–Mihaly Csikszentmihalyi

It's okay to have a favorite room in your Real Colors home. But you'll find more fulfillment overall if you learn to move freely throughout all the rooms. The ability to flow freely from Gold to Green, Blue to Orange, etc. not only helps you relate more to other people, it provides more balance in your day-to-day life. To understand this need for flow, let's consider how each color adds to your life.

COLOR	4-P's	4-P QUESTIONS
Blue	Purpose	What makes this important?
Gold	Parameters	What are the rules of the game?
Green	Process	How will I make this work?
Orange	Priorities	Will it make a difference?

The 4-P Questions
Figure 2.1

I like to think of the four colors in terms of what I have come to call the 4-P's (Johnson, 2003). Figure 2.1 lists each of these P's by color along with a question designed to guide your thinking as you apply the color to real-life situations.

Every human being is born with the capability of functioning in each of the four colors. In fact, it is impossible to function in life without addressing all of them. By thinking of the colors in terms of the 4-P's, you can begin to see how you need each.

Blue represents every human being's need to understand how things connect to a higher <u>purpose</u>. Blue represents the spiritual sense that is present to some degree in each of us. It addresses the Frankl question of meaning. It is the intuitive connection that links all life throughout the universe. It causes us to ask that deeper question of importance that leads to fit – how does what I am about to do fit with the spiritual principles that pervade our universe?

Gold represents every human being's attempt to manage or control the daily activities of life. Gold is a practical color that fences in a particular space according to certain <u>parameters</u>. It explains why a house has separate rooms. It makes it possible for us to say, "The kitchen is where I prepare my food so that I can sit in the dining room to eat with friends prior to adjourning to the living room to have a glass of sherry and chat." It compartmentalizes the "holistic" nature of purpose to manage day-to-day real-life functions. Gold raises a practical question of the rules of the game being played at any particular moment so that we can conserve resources.

⟲Interior Design in Your Real Colors Home

Green represents every human being's need to understand how things work and, more important, how "I" can make them work. Green represents the process, critical thinking aspect of life. Like Blue, Green is about connections, but Green focuses less on spiritual questions in favor of logical or scientific questions. How can I align my attitudes and what I do with other things going on in the universe so that I can gain the greatest leverage for my effort?

Orange represents every human being's attempt to seize the moment, to experience as many aspects of life as possible in the time allotted to us. Orange represents the desire to act on our world, to understand the priorities that enable us to effect change around us. Orange is as practical as Gold but less directed toward managing than discovering. Orange raises the practical question of risk and experimentation as a means of gathering more — nothing ventured, nothing gained.

Returning to our four-room house for a moment, let's consider some of the relationships that allow us to flow more freely from room to room. Figure 2.2 focuses on the similarities and differences between concretes — Gold and Orange.

If your primary color is Gold or Orange, you approach life from the practical side of your Real Colors home. It is not that Golds and Oranges don't realize that life has a purpose and that certain processes provide logical connections between and among life events. But concrete Golds and Oranges differ from the more abstract Blues and Greens in that they see little to connect

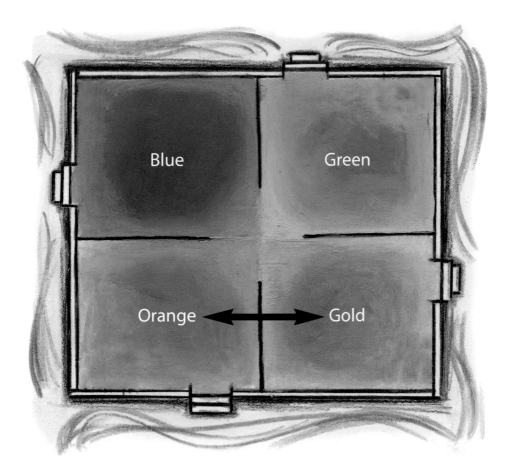

The Concrete Continuum
Figure 2.2

either spiritually or scientifically if someone doesn't tend the garden (Gold) or go looking for new food sources (Orange). Focusing on concrete aspects of life is about survival.

The difference between Golds and Oranges, on the other hand, is that Golds want to conserve what they have as opposed to looking for something else. The two words that describe these concrete poles are probability versus possibility. Figure 2.3 illustrates these poles through language that describes what I call Gold and Orange "comfort zones."

GOLD	ORANGE
I know that...	I wonder if...
I need to find...	I wish I could discover...
Close the door...	Open the doors and...
How do I protect...	How do I win...
The safest route...	The fastest route...
I have collected so many good...	I have the best...

Concrete Comfort Zones
Figure 2.3

If you look at each side of this figure, you will see aspects of yourself in both columns. But if you force yourself to choose between columns for each set of words, which one do you find yourself in most often? Now consider the strengths and liabilities of each one. There is great advantage to having a depth of knowledge in one field, but if you don't explore the world around you, life can become rather monotonous. Conversely, it is great to discover new worlds, but you won't get far without some knowledge of existing facts and skills. It is great to organize things so that they are easy to find, but if you spend too much time organizing what you have, you may miss doing something that you might have enjoyed even more. Conversely, if you are always looking for the next experience or thrill, you may never become skilled at anything. And the list continues.

The concept of flowing between and among rooms requires balance. Ask yourself where your life falls on the concrete continuum. And remember that the goal is not to maintain a static balance between Gold and Orange. It is to learn to recognize where you feel most comfortable. We all need to feel comfortable to avoid too much stress in our lives. But without some bit of dissonance from time to time it is impossible to learn and grow. Again, it is much easier to build from the positive, from an understanding and acceptance of who we are, than from the negative.

Let's take a quick concrete continuum quiz. Jot down your answer (Gold or Orange) to each of the following questions. Then explain your choice in a few words. You can check your answers at the end of this chapter.

QUESTION	COLOR	RATIONALE
1) What color was Ben Franklin when he said, "Neither a borrower nor a lender be"?		
2) What color was Horace Greeley when he said, "Go West, young man"?		
3) What color was Christopher Columbus when he set out on his now famous voyage?		
4) What color was King Ferdinand, who supported Columbus' voyage?		
5) What color was John Paul Jones when he said, "I have not yet begun to fight"?		

Concrete Continuum Quiz

Now let's shift our attention to the abstract side of our Real Colors home. Figure 2.4 focuses on the similarities and differences between abstracts – Blues and Greens.

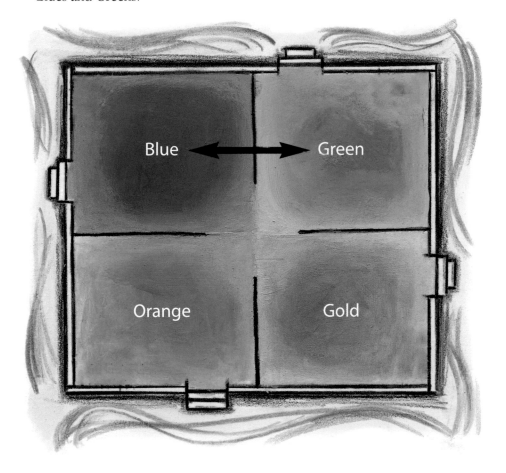

The Abstract Continuum
Figure 2.4

The abstract continuum is about connections. It could be said to run from connections among people (or life forms of any sort) to connections among principles – people versus ideas. Blues and Greens differ from the concrete Golds and Oranges in that they find little reason to engage with life if it offers little more than survival. To these Blue and Green abstracts, life without purposeful human relationships and an understanding of fundamental life processes is no life at all. Blues and Greens, in fact, tend to speak in hyperboles, seeming to recognize that their minority status in the world requires them to make grand statements of purpose and process.

Yet, like their concrete friends, not everything is totally harmonious between these abstract Blues and Greens. Blues focus on connections that make people's lives more pleasant and meaningful. Blues have a more immediate need for satisfaction than do Greens. Greens focus on connections that exist between and among all life events regardless of how pleasant or unpleasant they may be. Greens are willing to take time to contemplate. They think of themselves as having the ability to step back from a situation and consider all aspects objectively. Figure 2.5 illustrates these poles through language that describes the Blue and Green "comfort zones."

BLUE	GREEN
I want to understand if…	I want to know why…
I need to feel that…	I need to figure out why…
I love to spend time talking with friends about…	I enjoy having time alone to think about…
I could spend all day at a gallery…	I could spend all day at a museum…
There's nothing more comfortable than a glass of wine, a good friend, and a warm fire to…	There's nothing more relaxing than a glass of wine, a good puzzle, and symphonic music to…
I wish people took more time to…	I don't know why more people can't understand that…

Abstract Comfort Zones
Figure 2.5

As with the concrete continuum, if you look at each side of Figure 2.5, you will see aspects of yourself in both columns. But if you force yourself to choose between columns for each set of words, which one do you find yourself in most often? Now consider the strengths and liabilities of each one. There is great advantage in having rich human relationships, but if you don't take time to explore the principles underlying those relationships, you may find them difficult to duplicate. Conversely, it is great to figure out how relationships work, but you may become so absorbed in analyzing them that you fail to enjoy them. It is great to spend time with people, but if you spend too much time focusing on your relationships with others, you may fail to take enough time for yourself. Conversely, if you are always doing things alone to avoid distractions, you may find yourself totally self-absorbed and lacking positive friendships. And the list continues.

Ask yourself where your life falls on the abstract continuum. Again, the goal is not to maintain a static balance between Blue and Green. It is to learn to recognize where you feel most comfortable. How will you build from the positive, from an understanding and acceptance of where you are on the abstract continuum to where you might like to evolve? Evolution is generally easier than revolution.

Now it is time to take a quick abstract continuum quiz. This time, jot down your answer (Blue or Green) to each question. Then explain your choice in a few words. You can check your answers at the end of this chapter.

QUESTION	COLOR	RATIONALE
1) What color was William Shakespeare when he said, "All the world is a stage…"?		
2) What color was Mother Teresa when she said, "Love is a fruit in season at all times, and within reach of every hand"?		
3) What color was Rene Descartes when he said, "I think; therefore, I am"?		
4) What color was Edison when he spent years developing the light bulb?		
5) What color was Jack Kerouac's mother who supported him so that he could write his books?		

Abstract Continuum Quiz

⟲ Interior Design in Your Real Colors Home

Your Real Colors workshop presenter pointed out over and over that you cannot be certain of a person's colors simply on the basis of their actions. You need to understand the reasons underlying those actions. For example, teachers are primarily Golds (approximately 70 percent). They are effective technicians, logistical folks who can focus on and hone skills that they can teach to others. However, it is not enough to know that a person is a teacher to decide that they are Gold. Greens may go into teaching because they want to help children learn the joy of learning in and of itself. Blues may go into teaching as a means of introducing children to the creative world of possibilities. Oranges may go into teaching to ensure that kids aren't bored or misunderstood in school the way they were as students.

Numerous factors either enhance or impede the comfort and functionality of a home. This is also true of your Real Colors home. The walls of your Real Colors home are movable. Likewise, the amount of time you spend in each room is flexible. But how you design the rooms within your Real Colors home will affect how much you use them. Sometimes you simply can't get comfortable in a room because it is drafty. You may find that when you try to sit in your preferred Green room, you feel a draft coming from some other area of the house.

The draft may be coming from the Gold room – those past parental or teacher admonitions to quit being a loner, to be more of a team player, or to get your work done first and to play later. Or you may feel a draft coming from the Orange room – those past voices from coaches or playmates who laughed at you for being a nerd. And of course, the draft may be coming from the Blue room – that voice from your spouse who wants to hear about your day or your friend who can't understand why she never hears from you.

Are these voices simply annoyances, or are they warning calls? Only you can decide that. But at the very least, you don't have to sit in your preferred room (whatever the color) in fear that if you venture into another area, you will lose your way back to your favorite spot. The chances are that you would not be able to stay out of your preferred room if you tried. Many researchers tell us that our temperament never changes. I prefer to think of my temperament home as flexible. I may not change the way I enter my Real Colors home or even in which room(s) I spend most of my time. However, if I start to think about my less preferred rooms in terms of how they might complement my more preferred areas, I may find that they can become more pleasant and functional than I had realized they could be.

If you are an Orange who has been frequently criticized for your inability to be punctual or organized, you might try to think about the types of activities for which you are on time or for which you are willing to practice religiously. Then you can begin to think of those things that are important to you in terms of how order (and other Gold qualities) might enhance your Orange world. In other words, place some Orange objects in your Gold room or some Gold objects in your Orange room. Even the most competitive Orange can follow the rules of the game if they find the game challenging enough. You don't need to camp in the Gold room to enjoy its benefits. All it may require is moving some of your Orange paraphernalia out of the doorway to the Gold room so that it will be easier to flow back and forth.

The irony is that we often seek out people, especially as mates, who complement our temperament. For example, Doug is a Green who relies heavily on his Blue spouse to plan their social calendar, to help him maintain positive relationships with his children, and to make their home a place where people love to spend an evening. Jane is an Orange who relies on her Gold spouse to balance the checkbook, to make dinner reservations in advance, and to plan their vacations. On the other hand, Jane's husband is more than willing to have Jane choose their vacation destination and activities, knowing that she will choose fun and exciting events.

As you come to understand your pathways through your Real Colors home, you will also come to appreciate how others view your habits and how you can adjust those habits not simply to satisfy them, but to satisfy your own need for balance. By learning to ask the 4-P questions, you can identify your strengths and capitalize on them. You can also learn to identify your liabilities in order to minimize their negative impact on your life. And ultimately, as you learn to trust yourself more, you will find that you will invite people into your life who can help you take advantage of those underutilized rooms in your Real Colors home. The difference now, however, will be that they will be invited guests rather than pests or intruders.

In the next section of this guide, we will investigate ways of identifying what furniture you have in your Real Colors home and what pieces you may want to keep, reupholster, or discard. But first, take a moment to reflect on the following questions as a way of thinking about the interior design of your Real Colors home.

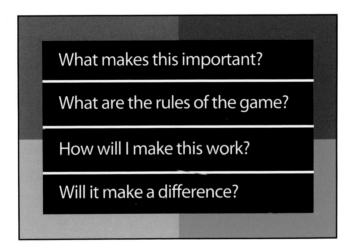

What makes this important?

What are the rules of the game?

How will I make this work?

Will it make a difference?

The 4-P Questions

1. How much time do you spend in each room of your Real Colors home?
   Blue _____ Gold _____ Green _____ Orange_____

2. To what degree do you find that lifestyle working for you? _____

   _____

   In terms of personal comfort? _____

   _____

   In terms of family relationships and friendships? _____

   _____

   In terms of work or career? _____

   _____

3. How much of the way you feel about the interior design of your Real
   Colors home is a factor of your personal desire for balance, and how
   much is a factor of guilt for not fulfilling someone else's expectations
   for you? _____

   _____

4. Where would you like to start your redecorating project? (Remember to
   start with your strength and ADD other colors.)

   My preferred color _____

   Strengths: _____

   My least preferred color _____

   Small signs of this color in my life that can be expanded include: _____

   _____

Remember that few incidents are purely one color. Also, be aware that the rationale column is a list of possible rationales that is neither absolute nor exhaustive.

Concrete Continuum Quiz

Question	Color	Rationale
1. What color was Ben Franklin when he said, "Neither a borrower nor a lender be"?	Gold	Golds are thrifty individuals who depend on their own hard work to get ahead.
2. What color was Horace Greeley when he said, "Go West, young man"?	Orange	Oranges want adventure and are willing to take risks.
3. What color was Christopher Columbus when he set out on his now famous voyage?	Orange	He needed to find out if the world was round even if it required risk.
4. What color was King Ferdinand, who supported Columbus' voyage?	Gold	These Golds had the money that the adventurous Columbus did not.
5. What color was John Paul Jones when he said, "I have not yet begun to fight"?	Orange	Jones was prepared to die in glory rather than to survive in defeat.

Abstract Continuum Quiz

Question	Color	Rationale
1. What color was William Shakespeare when he said, "All the world is a stage"?	Blue	Shakespeare saw both art and irony in life as he spoke in metaphors.
2. What color was Mother Teresa when she said, "Love is a fruit in season at all times, and within reach of every hand"?	Blue	Blues see the world as a positive experience for anyone who chooses to reach for it.
3. What color was Rene descartes when he said, "I think; therefore, I am"?	Green	Greens think that the essence in life originates in ideas and ideation.
4. What color was Edison when he spent years developing the light bulb?	Green	Greens are persistent in their desire to understand how things can work. (There is also some Orange risk-taking evident here.)
5. What color was Kerouac's mother who supported him so that he could write his books?	Blue	If guilt or worry drove Mother Kerouac, this was a Gold act. But if it was simply a matter of supporting her adult son as an artist, she was definitely Blue.

Taking an Inventory of Your Real Colors Stuff

⟲ Taking an Inventory of Your Real Colors Stuff

*"Have you ever noticed how much stuff
you can accumulate over the years?"*

– George Carlin

George Carlin has made us laugh about the "stuff" we collect over the years, some of it by chance and some of it by choice. He suggests that stuff (and our relationship to it) tells people a great deal about us — what stuff is important, why it is important, and how willing we are to share it. The same is true of your Real Colors stuff. Where did your Real Colors stuff come from? Did you pick it yourself? How much was a gift from someone else? When did you last use this stuff, and how much is still useful to you?

Having moved numerous times over the years, I know about sorting through "stuff." I am ever the saver, attaching inexplicable value to objects I haven't seen in 20 years. My wife, on the other hand, is a pitcher. To her, anything that hasn't seen the light of day in the previous 24 months belongs to charity. From time to time — especially prior to a move — my wife and I sit down to inventory our stuff in order to determine what should be saved, what needs repair, and what simply needs to be discarded. Generally we find that some stuff is easily sorted into the save or discard categories. But some stuff seems to defy sorting. It has no apparent value. We cannot remember where or how we came by it. Yet, somehow we simply cannot seem to part with it. These inventories don't necessarily explain all our value decisions, but at least they make our stuff more manageable.

Let's take a moment to review the kinds of stuff we might find in various rooms of our Real Colors home. Figure 3.1 lists stuff commonly found in a Blue room, a Gold room, etc.

Blue	**Green**
Art, CDs, Old love notes, Poetry, Telephone, Fireplace, Old birthday cards, Wine glasses	Computer, Computer games, Science magazines, Telescope, Birdwatcher's guide, Fax, Puzzle books, Stereo headphones
Gold	**Orange**
File cabinet, Table, Rolodex, Snack tray, Bookcase, Pencil sharpener, Notepad, Dictionary	Tennis racket, Golf clubs Keys to motorcycle, *Sports Illustrated*, Big screen television, Joke books, Snack food, Games

Where's My Stuff
Figure 3.1

⟲ Taking an Inventory of Your Real Colors Stuff

This figure contains an illustrative rather than an exhaustive list of stuff found in each room of your Real Colors home. Obviously, the items are not found exclusively in the rooms shown here. If you think of an object as belonging in a different room, remember to ask yourself the reasons behind your placement. Colors run deeper than objects and actions. They evolve from motivations. For example, you might want your fireplace in a different room – Gold to keep you warm or Orange to keep you busy. More important than where you place an object is why you placed it there.

To complete your Real Colors inventory, ask yourself about the stuff that affects your everyday world. Go beyond mere objects to the beliefs, attitudes, and habits that have become a part of you. How much has the Blue stuff in life affected who you are – the Gold, the Green, and the Orange? Which stuff carries negative baggage, regardless of the room that houses it? As you sort through your temperament stuff, ask yourself the following questions.

Inventory Questions

1) How much stuff have I collected in each room of my Real Colors home?

2) Where did my color stuff come from – parents, friends, work, personal choice, don't know?

3) How often and how effectively do I use my color stuff?

4) How comfortable do I feel when I use my color stuff?

5) How might a decision to use certain color stuff more or less affect movement throughout my Real Colors home?

Begin your inventory by revisiting your color preferences. Which color is most like you — which next, next, and least? I call this your color "order." Again, if you are Blue, your primary focus is on issues of purpose — connections among human beings and concepts that transcend physical or scientific explanations. If you are Gold, you focus primarily on parameters — those concrete, day-to-day objects and events and how they fit into manageable predetermined categories. If you are Green, you focus primarily on processes — underlying connections among ideas and principles that affect everyday lives over time. If you are Orange, you focus primarily on priorities — those concrete objects and events that are most readily available and hold the greatest potential to bring about the immediate desired results.

How much stuff have I collected in each room of my Real Colors home?

As mentioned earlier in this guide, the extent to which we identify ourselves Blue, Gold, Green, or Orange varies even among people of the same color order. Any single incident or relationship can be categorized in a number of different ways, depending on the people involved and various aspects of the situation. As you read through the following descriptions of "stuff," try to focus on their general characteristics in terms of clarifying and differentiating between and among the colors. These examples are meant to be illustrations rather than precise definitions.

⟳ Taking an Inventory of Your Real Colors Stuff

Blue Stuff

Art, for example, can be collected in various ways. If I love art and am surrounded by family and friends who love art, I am likely to gain a deep and meaningful understanding of art. If I am exposed to art at school, have access to art museums, and am encouraged to create my own art, my appreciation of art will grow even further.

On the other hand, if my family and friends don't appreciate art, laugh at me for my interest in art, and try to interest me in non-art stuff, I am not as likely to have collected the art I would like to have. In fact, I may feel guilty or stupid for having such art interests. At the very least, I will probably not act on my art interests in the same way that I would have if my interests had been reinforced. Unfortunately for me, schools and businesses that promote art are scarce in our society.

Gold Stuff

Bank accounts, cars, homes, and similar durable goods can be collected in similar fashion. If I have a desire to collect and organize "durable goods" and am surrounded by family and friends who encourage and reward such behavior, I am likely to view success as collecting lots of "durable" stuff. I will probably feel inadequate or unsuccessful if I don't collect enough durable stuff.

On the other hand, if my family and friends lack an interest in collecting durable stuff, I may learn to feel guilty about my "obsession" with it. At the very least, I will find it more difficult to gather stuff, since it takes stuff (money or collateral) to get other stuff. Fortunately for me, however, schools and businesses emphasize management and durable stuff and will reward my efforts early in life.

Green Stuff

Science, for example, is used to figure out how other stuff works. It might include microscopes, computers, and books about systems and processes. If I live near a science museum, attend a school that focuses on mathematics and science, and am surrounded by people who encourage me to question and wonder, I will probably collect a lot of science stuff.

On the other hand, if my family, friends, and teachers discourage me from taking stuff apart, from asking too many "silly" questions, or from wanting to play with a computer game rather than a baseball, I may not develop the same sense of wonder or depth of understanding that my Blue, Gold, or Orange counterparts would gain. I may come to think of myself as a nerd. Unfortunately, teachers and parents talk a great deal about scientific thinking, but real world events don't reward it in childhood.

⟳ Taking an Inventory of Your Real Colors Stuff

Orange Stuff

Orange stuff is designed for people who enjoy competition and adventure. Oranges are likely to love games and entertainment – sports, for example. If my family can afford to take me to sporting events, encourage me to participate in sporting events, and support me even when I make mistakes, I will probably take risks and come to see mistakes as learning opportunities. If I am fortunate enough to have patient elementary teachers who can overlook my enthusiasm and fidgeting, I may survive to become quite a star in high school sports.

On the other hand, if my family is impatient with my failure to make my bed, finish my chores, and get things done on time, I may come to see myself as a klutz. If my teachers can't cope with my abundant energy, scold me for my lack of attention, and deny me recess when my work is incomplete, I may come to think of myself as dumb. Unfortunately, the friends who share my interest in risk taking and adventure actually reinforce the very behaviors that my teachers seem to abhor.

Where did my color stuff come from?

Some Real Colors workshop participants ask if colors change over time. Otherwise, why would almost all children seem to be curious, fidgety, and willing to take risks while most adults learn to be more mannerly, attentive, and conservative. Perhaps the explanation is not all that complicated. Will, a father and grandfather, put it this way: "You don't become conservative until you have something to conserve." Again, actions don't identify colors. Underlying reasons or motivations do. While the intensity of individual colors may change over time, most temperament theorists agree that our color order does not.

If you have a natural tendency to collect Blue stuff and you are surrounded by others who appreciate Blue stuff, you are likely to feel comfortable with yourself. However, you may become so accustomed to Blue stuff that you find it boring at times. In fact, you may collect so much Blue stuff that it clutters your Blue room and spills into other rooms. Your lack of time and attention to anything that is not Blue may inhibit your ability to appreciate other colors. In time you may even find that other people don't like to be around you because your Blue stuff gets in their way.

This is what we mean when we say that each color has its strengths and liabilities. This also explains what we mean when we say that a liability is often little more than a strength that we carry too far. Social misfits are likely to raise social misfits, regardless of their color. Balanced adults are likely to raise balanced children, regardless of their color. What we fail to consider at times, however, are the factors that either encourage or discourage balance.

⟲ Taking an Inventory of Your Real Colors Stuff

If parents have not collected adequate Gold stuff, there is little Gold for them to share with their children. If parents were discouraged from being Orange or failed to gather all the Orange stuff that they had dreamed of, they may be unable or unwilling to pass it on to their children. And so go the ironies of life.

We can't pass on something we never owned.

Imagine for a moment that you are an Orange child whose parents have both filled their lives with a lot of Gold stuff. Even if they give you opportunities to learn for yourself, and even if you are a highly skilled Orange, you are going to make mistakes. And when you make those mistakes, your parents will probably use them as examples of why your behavior is "careless" and "risky," why it is "better to be safe than sorry."

Or imagine yourself to be a Gold whose risk-taking friend "hits the jackpot" with one of his risky schemes. As you look around, you begin to notice others who have made it big without going to college, without saving for retirement, and without spending money on life and accident insurance. Suddenly you begin to question why you are so Gold. You wonder if there is truly any virtue in hard work and careful planning. But are these examples the rule or the exception?

Much of what we believe or accept as comfortable or right comes from our own ability to reason and evaluate personal or vicarious experiences. However, much of it comes from other voices — parents, teachers, friends —

in subtle, almost undetectable forms. It is a good idea to look at our Real Colors stuff from time to time to determine where it comes from.

How often and how effectively do I use my color stuff?

A good way to develop balance in your Real Colors home is to ask how effectively you use your color stuff. Are you a Blue who uses Blue effectively? Do you recognize when it is appropriate to take some of your Blue stuff into the Gold room to be organized, or do you simply allow it to pile up in the Blue room. Have you expanded your Blue room to the point that you no longer have much space in the Gold room? Or have your parents, friends, or responsibilities caused you to expand the Gold room to the point that you have little space left to put the Blue stuff you want?

Let's assume for a moment that you are Green with a follow-up Orange. This color combination is quite effective in inventing something new. Your primary Green allows you to figure out the connections or principles involved in situations, and your follow-up Orange allows you to remain open to numerous options. And these "invention" skills are not limited to objects. Green-Orange is an ideal color combination for negotiations – inventing creative solutions to human relations problems.

However, if you don't allow
yourself to exercise
your Gold and Blue
from time to time,
you may find that
people begin to view
you as a manipulator or
an opportunist. "She doesn't

have any real convictions (Gold). All she wants to do is
be the hero." Or, "She doesn't care about me as a person (Blue). All she
wants to do is solve her problem."

If we want to get along with others and maintain balance in our own life, we
need to "do" all the colors. Without Gold, our Green-Orange might try to
take on every problem (the fixer). Without Blue, Green-Oranges can lose
sight of purpose, forgetting why something was worth doing in the first
place. Like exercising our muscles, we need to exercise our colors regularly.
Walkers often develop strong leg muscles but experience lower back pain
because their stronger leg muscles pull too hard against their weaker back
muscles. Over-exercising our color preference can leave us weak in other
important areas.

How comfortable do I feel when I use my color stuff?

There are two fundamental factors that affect your sense of comfort with your color order:

The reactions that you receive over time from other people when you function through various colors and

How appropriately you have learned to balance your preferred color with other colors in various situations.

If parents, friends, and significant others have reacted favorably to your "personality or style" over time, you will probably feel comfortable exercising that color. On the other hand, if you have never been able to do that "touchy-feely" stuff, for example, you will probably be reticent to employ your Blue. People who are unappreciated for their Blue sometimes over-compensate by being boisterous or defensive. Others may become shy or withdrawn.

And are you one of those people whom people seem to appreciate at a first meeting but shy away from later? Perhaps you have never mastered the art of timing or the knack of reaching out through someone else's color. People may appreciate an Orange's sense of humor but find it overbearing when that Orange "doesn't know when to get serious" or can't pick-up cues well enough to know that their Orange sense of humor does not suit circumstances at a given moment. People may appreciate a sensitive Blue in a social gathering but find them naive in a problem-solving situation. People may appreciate a Green's ability to be objective and singularly focused in

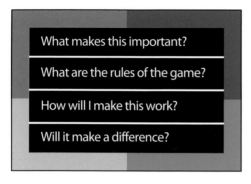

The 4-P Questions

a problem-solving situation but find them impersonal or monotonous in a social situation. Be certain to ask yourself the 4-P questions. And ask yourself what the situation in which you find yourself calls for. Identify the color of the moment and start there.

How might a decision to use certain color stuff more or less affect movement throughout my Real Colors home?

If you are comfortable with your color order, you are much more likely to balance the colors effectively. You will see the balance that your preferred color brings to the table, and you will understand how people and circumstances change to require more or less of it. When you recognize that someone's failure to appreciate your color stuff may be as much a factor of the situation as it is of your color versus their color, you become less defensive and more willing to make your point through a different color or approach. You may even improve your flexibility in responding to others and find them more willing to adjust, in turn, to your color needs. You can learn to adapt to another person's color needs without abandoning your color preference.

Once you no longer equate a color with negative past experiences, you can appreciate how it fits into your color order and how your color order matches the situation in which you find yourself. Figure 3.2 illustrates this point.

My Color Needs   Your Color Needs

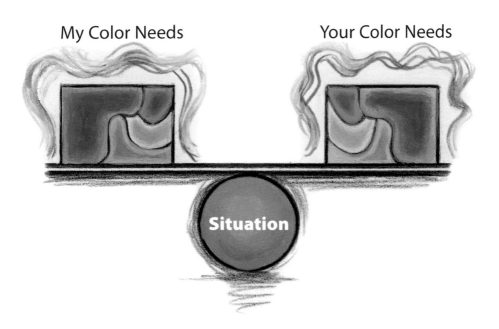

Balancing My Color Needs With Yours
Figure 3.2

As you become more sensitive to these balancing forces, you will find that you can flow more freely from one color to another without losing sight of who you are and what you want from a situation. For example, a Blue may be interested in art, but a Blue-Orange might be more open to new art forms than would a Blue-Gold. A potential Blue-Orange artist might be extremely talented but less likely than a Blue-Gold to take the necessary time to develop a technique through practice. On the other hand, the Blue-Gold might be less capable than a Blue-Orange of "shipping" his work, i.e. recognizing it as salable if not absolutely perfect. Only you can determine the extent to which your comfort can be sacrificed temporarily to achieve a long-term goal. But if you don't take the time to inventory your Real Colors stuff and recognize when to call on all your colors appropriately, you may be missing an opportunity to choose your course rather than reacting to choices that someone else has made for you.

Stephen R. Covey (1989) encourages us to "seek first to understand and then to be understood." At first glance this admonition may seem to encourage people to place their own needs behind the needs of others. But by following Covey's adage, you can also serve your needs. Sometimes we can get a different perspective of ourselves by understanding how others see us. Likewise, by recognizing and respecting other people's stuff, we increase the likelihood that they will eventually notice (and hopefully respect) our stuff.

In the next chapter of this guide, we will look at ways to decide what stuff you want to keep for your new Real Colors home and what stuff you might wish to discard. But before we go there, let's take a moment to reflect on your Real Colors inventory.

1. What is the order of your color rainbow? _____

2. Given your Real Colors workshop experience and what you have read in this chapter, make a list of the stuff (attitudes, beliefs, etc.) that you have collected in each of your Real Colors rooms.

   Blue _____
   Green _____
   Gold _____
   Orange _____

3. Underline the stuff above that you put in your house. Circle stuff that parents, friends, and co-workers gave you. Where did anything else come from?

4. How much do you use the stuff you included in your inventory? _____

   _____

5. What stuff are you going to keep or expand in each of the four rooms of your house?

   Blue _____
   Green _____
   Gold _____
   Orange _____

6. Is there anything in any of these four rooms that you want to discard? If so, what and why?

   Blue _____
   Green _____
   Gold _____
   Orange _____

The Right Real Colors Home for You

⟲ The Right Real Colors Home for You

*"Having too many things, they spend their hours
and money on the couch searching for a soul."*

–Adlai Stevenson

Happiness is often hard to find. Once found, it is fleeting. Once past, it is hard to replicate. It seems to appear when we least expect it, and if we are worried and focused on a problem, happiness may walk past our door unnoticed.

You aren't likely to find a surefire pathway to happiness. Happiness does not appear as an epiphany, and you know that it often eludes millionaires. But Real Colors can help you understand your temperament. It helps you feel better about who you are and to balance how you want to live your life in relationship to others. This balance, in turn, makes it possible for you to recognize happiness when it approaches and to appreciate it however briefly it may linger.

Once you understand various Real Colors floor plans and inventory your Real Colors stuff, you can decide on the right Real Colors home for you. Decisions about choosing the right Real Colors home are similar to decisions about choosing a home for your family. If you lack enough resources for a down payment, you may decide to rent until you can set more money aside. If you have adequate savings for a down payment, you have the option of buying or building.

Your Real Colors workshop presenter gave you the renter's guide to Real Colors homes. The workshop was a way of experiencing temperament first-hand. After the workshop, you may have taken your color cards home and tried them on friends and family. But given the fact that you picked up this guide, you obviously want to learn more. If you are an adult, you may feel that your Real Colors home has been built according to other people's specifications, and now you want to remodel or add onto it to make it suit your needs. Obviously, the younger you are when you learn about your colors and the more support you have from family and friends in developing your own color balance, the greater your chances will be of designing and building the Real Colors home that is right for you.

Let's take a moment to consider the stuff that you want to put in your Real Colors home. When you inventoried your Real Colors stuff in the last chapter, how much of it was stuff you chose for yourself? How much was something someone else gave you, and how useful is it to you today? And finally, whether you chose it or it was given to you, is there anything that you want to get rid of or replace? It can be exciting to choose new stuff for your new home, but it may be helpful to have a garage sale first.

After inventorying her Real Colors stuff, Terry found some things that her parents had given her that she no longer found useful. Like most parents, Terry's mother and father had meant to be helpful in sharing their view of the world with Terry. However, as Terry learned to appreciate her own Blue-Orange view of the world, she realized that her inability to gather more Gold and Green as her parents had encouraged her to do, was not as big of a problem as she had come to believe. Although Terry's parents are both deceased now, she might benefit from writing the following letter.

Dear Mom and Dad,

I've recently purchased my own home and have been going through some of my stuff. It is absolutely amazing how much of that stuff I got from you. Wow, Dad, you were always insisting that I try to be more logical and less dramatic. I actually have a lot of Green stuff; thanks to you. And Mom, you always told me to be more organized and on time. Wow, I can't believe the amount of Gold stuff that you caused me to collect over the years.

I've used your Green stuff, Dad, to earn a degree in fashion design. And Mom, I've used the Gold stuff you gave me as an incentive to learn the rules of the clothing business. Thanks for giving me all that you had to give. I'm certainly better for it today.

But now I am working in fashion design, and guess what? They love my creativity and appreciate the fact that no two of my dress designs are ever the same. In fact, that is what makes them so expensive and me about to become so rich – or at least self-sufficient. And you know what else? I am happier than I have ever been in my life because my company has learned to deal with me as I am – maybe because I have learned to deal with who I am.

Anyhow, instead of giving me a design room and having me move to their London-based offices, the company has given me an allowance to buy the equipment I need for my in-home office. They also allow me to e-mail and fax design ideas. Then once every month or six weeks, I fly to London (it's a dirty job, but someone has to do it) and we adjust the designs with their models and consultants.

So, I'm keeping some of the Green and Gold stuff you guys gave me – thanks. But I need to send some of it back to you to make room for the Blue and Orange stuff I need in my new job. I've been shopping, and I never realized how much Blue and Orange stuff there is in the world and how much other people like it. I only wish I had been able to describe it better to you guys when I was growing up. I think you might have enjoyed it, too.

Your more balanced daughter,

Terry

⟳ The Right Real Colors Home for You

Few parents stay awake at night conjuring up ways to make their children's lives miserable. In fact, most parents believe they are doing the right thing when they try to teach their children "better" life-skills. After all, there is nothing worse than an ill-mannered child – right? And if children don't learn to be more_____ (we can fill in the blank with whatever skill we consider them to be lacking), they certainly won't get ahead in this world.

And child-rearing "mistakes" are not always a factor of parents being at odds with their children. Jeff is a Green-Gold whose parents are both Green-Golds. Even though he has remodeled his Real Colors home to increase the size of his Green room, Jeff finds himself as an adult with an exceptionally large amount of Green stuff strewn throughout his home. Jeff might like to send the following letter to his parents.

Dear Mom and Dad,

I've been contemplating my Green world lately. Wow, between all the Green stuff you guys have given me over the years and the Green stuff I've collected myself, I find I have very little room for any other stuff at all. I seem to have become so obsessed with making certain that everything in my world is logical and orderly that I'm not certain I know how to enjoy myself anymore. And you know what? That girl I dated a few years ago – I think I should have married her when she asked me. I have my Ph.D. now and a great job in computer engineering, but I'm actually a pretty lonely guy.

And you know what else? My company is going under, and several other companies tell me that I'm over-qualified for any jobs they have. What's worse is that I don't have many other skills, and people seem to have a difficult time warming up to me.

So, I've decided to sell some of my Green and Gold stuff to make room for other things in my life. I'm having a garage sale and thought I'd invite you guys to bring some of your Gold and Green stuff to sell, too. You'd be surprised how much fun that Orange stuff can be, and Blue stuff really brings a sense of meaning to an otherwise bland home. There's not much chance of the three of us running out of Gold and Green stuff even if we have a great garage sale.

Anyhow, think about joining me. It could be a new experience for all of us.

Your more balanced son,

Jeff

⟲ The Right Real Colors Home for You

When parents or employers see their children or employees doing "good" things, they want to encourage and reinforce them. But if "good" things are defined as those things that feel comfortable to parents, friends, and employers, they may actually be short-changing children or employees in the same way that they have short-changed themselves in business decisions or in any other aspect of life. This is true for all colors but particularly noteworthy for Blues and Greens who already find themselves in the minority. We aren't necessarily helping Blues and Greens if we only support their Blue and Green actions without helping them appreciate and "do" Gold and Orange in order to interact more successfully with others.

As you read Jeff's letter, you may notice that he sounds lonely or perhaps lost. Blues and Greens are often valued for their unique ability to make connections, but they are also often criticized or even ridiculed for being different. When parents don't encourage their children to experience all colors of stuff, they risk creating individuals who lack balance and miss the adventure that life has to offer. When life becomes either too predictable or too unpredictable, it loses something, no matter what color(s) we may be. But it is never too late to find new color experiences. Let's consider how you can become more aware of the color that enters your world and more capable of engaging with it rather than reacting to it.

Watching for Color Clues in Words and Actions

Let's think about how people provide us clues to their color through their words and actions. Remember, these are clues – not absolute markers. We'll discuss listening for the questions behind the questions at a later point.

When a Blue is pleased...	When a Blue is agitated...
What would you like to do today?	Why can't people be more understanding about...?
How do you feel about that picture?	I thought his little tirade was childish and unforgivable.
Don't you just love that...?	All he cares about is his checkbook.
Don't you wish everyone took more time to...?	Doesn't he realize he could catch more flies with honey?
Wow, I just can't believe how you...	He's become little more than a mean-spirited...
I just love bird-watching with you. As a matter of fact, I love doing anything with you.	It's easier for me to pretend he simply doesn't exist.
Look at that sunset. Isn't nature awesome?	He wouldn't recognize kindness if it hit him in the face.

Listening for Blue Clues
Figure 4.1

Figure 4.1 lists words that are often clues for Blue. Remember, Blues place a premium on people and relationships.

Blue words generally include references to purpose and connections. As you listen for Blue clues, listen for connections with people and nature. Listen for a sense of awe about life itself. And don't be fooled into thinking that Blues are weak or never capable of wrath. Blues want to connect with others, but that connection needs to be peaceful and harmonious. Blues often test the waters with their words. Their tone, if not their words themselves, tends to be questioning and inviting. The more open-ended a Blue's question or comment, the more likely that their follow-up color is Orange. For example, a Blue-Orange might say, "Wow, I just can't believe how you..." Whereas, a Blue-Gold might say, "Don't you wish everyone took more time to...?"

When Blues are agitated, they may at first lament their situation: "Why can't people be more understanding about...?" As they grow more agitated, they can become more personal in their indignation: "I thought his little tirade was childish and unforgivable." And when they become totally exasperated, they might say, "It's easier for me to pretend he simply doesn't exist. The world would be a better place without this person." Blues tend to be extremely personal both in their praise and in their wrath. Now let's look for Gold clues.

When a Gold is pleased...	When a Gold is agitated...
Let's get our work finished or we can't…	Why can't people be more responsible when it comes to…?
That picture is a great example of Renaissance art. Notice the…	Someone needs to boot him in the pants when he tries one of his little tirades.
You need to spend more time…	I wish just once you would balance the checkbook.
I wish more people realized how dedicated you are to…	Forget all that honey stuff. I'd like to catch him by the throat and…
Wow, you certainly are one of the most responsible employees I have.	Someone needs to expose him for the mean-spirited person he is.
More than five species of birds have appeared here over the past three months.	After all the kind things we have done for him, you would think he could show some appreciation for…
Look at that sunset. Let's plan to have our coffee on the porch every night.	

Listening for Gold Clues
Figure 4.2

Figure 4.2 lists words that are often clues for Gold. Remember, Gold is about parameters and managing the situation.

Gold words generally include references to time management and parameters. As you listen for Gold clues, listen for rules and specific mention of responsibility. Listen for a need for order about life itself. But don't be fooled into thinking that Golds are impersonal or uncaring.

Golds see rules and order as a way of protecting everyone's rights, and they find it hard to imagine that everyone cannot appreciate management as a tool for reaching this softer, more esoteric side of life. Golds expect the waters to be calm and comfortable. They test them only to be certain that they are properly prepared. Their tone tends to be authoritative and based on givens. Golds are uncomfortable with situations that are open-ended. When they focus their questions or comments on people, their follow-up color is more likely to be Blue. For example, a Gold-Blue might say, "You need to spend more time...," as an admonition for you to take better care of yourself. Whereas a Gold-Green might say, "Let's get our work finished or we can't..." Here the focus is on work and rules – what we can't do unless we do something else.

When Golds are agitated, they may lament the lack of order in a situation: "Why can't people be more responsible when it comes to...?" As they grow more agitated, they can become more indignant: "Someone needs to expose him for the mean-spirited person he is." And when they become totally exasperated, they might say, "Forget all that honey stuff. I'd like to catch him by the throat and..." Golds focus on justice both in their praise and in their wrath. You earn their praise or their wrath. Now let's look for Green clues.

When a Green is pleased...	When a Green is agitated...
I think we ought to look at this situation more closely...	If people only realized...
What do you think of the artist's attempt to...?	I guess when you aren't smart enough to reason through something, you have to resort to childish tirades.
Don't you just love the way the rhythm of that song complements the words?	He should spend less time on his checkbook and more on his budget.
It only stands to reason that if more people took the time to...	I'm not interested in catching flies, and honey is sticky and disgusting.
You amaze me with your ability to...	I've noticed that anytime he isn't in charge, he becomes almost mean-spirited.
As I've catalogued the birds in this area, I've noticed that...	He does not think; therefore, he is not.
Were you aware that when the sun strikes the dust in the desert air...?	

Listening for Green Clues
Figure 4.3

Figure 4.3 lists clues for Green. Remember, Greens prefer to interact with the world using logic, process, and facts.

Green is about process and logic, and their Green words generally include references to process and logic.

As you listen for Green clues, listen for connections with ideas and principles. Listen for a sense of awe about how things work. And don't be fooled into thinking that Greens are insensitive and impersonal. Greens want to connect with others, but that connection needs to be logical and balanced. Greens think there would be little reason for strife if people were less emotional and more reasonable. Their tone, if not their words themselves, tends to be questioning and exploratory. The more open-ended a Green's question or comment, the more likely that their follow-up color is Orange. For example, a Green-Orange might say, "What do you think of the artist's attempt to…?" Whereas a Green-Gold might say, "It only stands to reason that if more people took the time to…"

When Greens are agitated, they seem to reason out loud: "If people only realized…" As they grow more agitated, they may express their indignation through sarcasm: "I guess when you aren't smart enough to reason through something, you have to resort to childish tirades." And when they become totally exasperated, they might say, "He does not think; therefore, he is not." Their words become cold and somewhat arrogant. Greens tend to be extremely logical and specific both in their praise and in their wrath.

When an Orange is pleased...	When an Orange is agitated...
Hey, I know! Let's…	Why can't people just…
That's a fantastic picture.	Man, she was ticked.
How could anyone not love…?	That guy never parts with a buck. No wonder he's so grumpy.
Life's too short. People need to…	The heck with catching flies. Spray the suckers.
Man, you are great. I've never seen anyone do that before.	Someone ought to teach that jerk a lesson.
Bird-watching is okay, but I prefer hunting birds.	Hey, does anyone here know a good hit man?
Look at that sunset. A beautiful end to an exciting day.	The kindest thing he could do is to shut his face.

Listening for Orange Clues
Figure 4.4

Figure 4.4 lists words that are often clues for Orange. Remember, Oranges place a priority on openness and adventure.

Orange words generally include references to fun and place a priority on immediacy. Notice the length of each Orange entry compared to the other colors.

You may not need to listen as closely for Orange clues, since they are usually direct and obvious. Listen for a sense of adventure. And don't be fooled into thinking that Oranges are simply flighty or unfocused. Oranges see fun and adventure as the primary means of connecting with others. A little risk makes life worth living. Oranges seldom test the waters with their words. They are about action. To an Orange, experience is the best teacher. Their tone and words tend to be exciting and unequivocal. The more emotional Oranges may focus on their Blue follow-up color through hyperbole. For example, an Orange-Blue might say, "That's a fantastic picture." Whereas, an Orange-Green might say, "Bird-watching is okay, but I prefer hunting birds." Note the seeming lack of sensitivity and the need for action.

When Oranges are agitated, they may use humor to make their point: "That guy never parts with a buck. No wonder he's so grumpy." As they grow more agitated, their humor becomes more pointed, more action oriented, and more sarcastic: "The heck with catching flies. Spray the suckers." And when they become totally exasperated, they might say, "The kindest thing he could do is to shut his face." An Orange's wrath often involves more bellicose language and physical challenge.

⑤ The Right Real Colors Home for You

Sometimes it is easier to recognize colors in others than it is to recognize them in yourself. Listen to people's words and ask questions. As you become more adept at recognizing their colors, turn your focus inward. At the same time, it is important to note that words, and even actions, can be deceiving. Let's take a moment to examine the message behind the words.

Probing Beyond Initial Color Clues

Sometimes the same word or action can emerge from entirely different motivations. We all develop defense mechanisms: avoiding painful situations, warding off pain through anger and harsh words, etc. A Blue who has never been appreciated for her Blueness may sound rather impersonal at times. Blue-Oranges, in particular may abandon normal pleasantries quickly when they sense that they are vulnerable or under attack. Your Real Colors workshop presenter may have referred to this condition as "being out of esteem." Unappreciated Golds, for example, may decide that following the rules has gotten them nowhere. They may decide that they have no choice but to shape the rules to achieve their unmet needs.

In most situations when individuals abandon their natural color tendencies, they blame their actions on those around them. Whether or not this blame is appropriately placed is unimportant. Until we recognize that we can either lament about how others created our situation or decide to change it ourselves, we will probably have difficulty getting rid of the color "stuff" that no longer serves our needs. Again, you can use your abstract-concrete or concrete-abstract combination to gain a broader perspective of who you are across the color continuum.

Jason was a very successful Green-Orange leader who worked in an organization that seemed to attract Gold-Blues. Having grown up in a home where his Gold father criticized his lack of order and carelessness and his Blue mother bemoaned his lack of concern for others, Jason spent much of his early career trying to change the Golds and Blues at work. Then he began to resent them for sounding like his parents. He even blamed them for his inability to accomplish his goals.

One day at work, a Gold co-worker asked Jason what he wanted to accomplish with a particular project. After a 30-minute oration from Jason, his patient co-worker said, "Would it be fair to say that the three things you want to achieve are...?" And immediately Jason realized how vague his plan was. But when he began to berate himself for his lack of logic, his co-worker said, "You have to be kidding me. I wish I could see the big picture the way you do. I can see the logistical details, but I need you to paint the picture for me. Hey, we could make a pretty effective team if we just had someone who could teach both of us to be a little more sensitive to people's feelings."

Jason's co-worker took the time to see beyond Jason's lack of detail. He recognized that Jason brought one set of skills to the table and that he came to that same table with a different, yet equally valuable, set. What Jason's co-worker was also aware of was that both he and Jason lacked the Blue tools so necessary for making the human connections involved in most problem-solving situations.

To learn more about others, you might say...

1) Wow, I never thought about it that way.

2) You know, you always have such a unique way of looking at things. Tell me more about…

3) I've heard you say that several times. Do you think…?

4) I think I have a good idea here, but I'm not the best person to figure out the details. Could you give me your advice on…?

5) I heard someone else say that, too. Why do you think…?

6) You know, Jack, I think sometimes I make you angry when I… Can you help me understand your concerns about this?

7) I wish I could _____ the way you do. Where did you learn that skill?

8) You know, with your (Color) and my (Color) we make a good team. Do you think either one of us could ever learn to…?

9) How important do you really think (relationships, order, etc.) really are in this situation?

Genuine Probing
Figure 4.5

The questions and statements in Figure 4.5 can help you gain a better understanding of people's temperament without making them feel unappreciated or manipulated.

These probes may help you identify color strengths and liabilities in the people around you. As you come to appreciate these differences, you should also become more comfortable with your own Real Colors stuff.

Then you can make better decisions about which stuff you want to keep and which you want to discard. The best rule of thumb is to be honest, caring, and genuine in your inquiry. Probing beyond initial color clues requires patient and repeated observations. It also requires an ability to ask questions that neither pry into personal business nor imply any sense of prejudgment.

How much of the stuff you have accumulated over the years will fit into your new Real Colors home, and what new stuff will you want to buy? Remember, no one ever develops the absolute right balance of color stuff. What works for one person may not work for someone else. Your Real Colors home needs to fit your needs.

Before we consider how you can balance your own needs with the needs of other people in your life, let's take a moment to reflect. Use your answers to the following questions to guide your Real Colors home choices.

1. List your color rainbow in order again. Has it changed as you have taken the time to inventory your Real Colors stuff and consider your remodeling needs? _____

   _____

   _____

   _____

   _____

   _____

   _____

2. Do you want to write a letter to anyone giving back some Real Colors things they have given you? Or do you want to invite anyone to a Real Colors garage sale? Write your thoughts here. _____

   _____

   _____

   _____

   _____

   _____

3. What common Real Colors clues have you heard from friends and acquaintances? Write them by color below.

   Blue _____

   Green _____

   Gold _____

   Orange _____

4. How do you know these clues represent the color you have indicated? Have you probed to understand the motives underlying these clues?

_____

5. What problems are you experiencing as you probe for the question behind the question? Are you remembering to be genuine and honest in posing your questions?

_____

_____

_____

_____

_____

_____

_____

_____

_____

_____

_____

_____

_____

Real Colors Home Improvement

⑤Real Colors Home Improvement

Dream it; design it; do it.

–The Home Depot

Now that you have selected the right Real Colors home design, you are ready to begin your home improvement project. The Home Depot assures customers that if they can dream it, The Home Depot can help them design and complete any home improvement project. As you gather your Real Colors tools, think about those things you've always wanted to do but have lacked the courage or support to try. Perhaps they involve letting go of an old attitude, improving relationships with family, friends, or people at work, or simply moving beyond guilt.

Most of us dream about things we want to be different in our lives, but now you have the tools you need to make your dream a reality. You have a design, and you have sorted through the colors of your life that add to or detract from your temperament balance. You have a target, and you know the temperament stuff you want to keep as you move into the future. Now as The Home Depot slogan above suggests, you need to "do it."

The next several pages of this guide are designed to help you execute an ongoing Real Colors renovation and maintenance plan. Consider this a guided practice through a four-step process.

1) Clean-up and minor repairs.
2) Recalibrating your temperament thermostat.
3) Adjusting Real Colors acoustics.
4) Conducting an open house.

We won't go into great detail in terms of specific relationships here – family relationships, work relationships, or similar topics. You can explore them in more depth in future Real Colors guides. For now, take a deep breath, gather your temperament tools, and have some fun with your own Real Colors home improvement project.

Step 1   Clean-up and Minor Repairs

At the beginning of this guide, you became familiar with the general Real Colors floor plan consisting of four rooms – one for each of the four colors. You considered how you may have developed skills and characteristics that felt comfortable and tended to lose sight of other ways of thinking about your world. You identified the larger room in your home (your first color preference) and considered how you may have chosen friends and career paths that meshed with or complemented your comfort zones – Greens become more Green, Golds become more Gold, etc.

You also considered what happens when parents, family, friends, and work responsibilities get in the way of your preferred color, limiting your ability to balance your desire to be your preferred color with your need to do all of the colors. You identified ways in which your natural temperament tendencies can be overshadowed by those cold drafts emanating from other rooms, causing you to close off the very doors that offered balance within your Real Colors home.

Figure 5.1 shows a comparison of these two situations – too much or too little of a good thing. Both floor plans in this figure represent the same color order: Green-Orange-Blue-Gold. (Larger rooms represent a stronger tendency toward a color; smaller rooms represent less comfort or use of that color.) Even with similar temperaments, interactions with parents, family, and friends, as well as critical life experiences, tend to shape people differently. The Real Colors floor plan at the top of this figure represents a person whose interactions and experiences have not supported a Green-Orange-Blue-Gold color order. The floor plan at the bottom represents a person whose interactions and experiences have supported a Green-Orange-Blue-Gold color order.

Notice that neither floor plan depicts a perfect color balance. The bottom plan is far preferable to the top; although the colors are not equal, this plan allows full movement among all of the colors. The Gold influences (represented within the dotted line) on the top plan are blocking the internal doorways that allow a person to move freely among the four colors.

Which design is most similar to your current temperament?

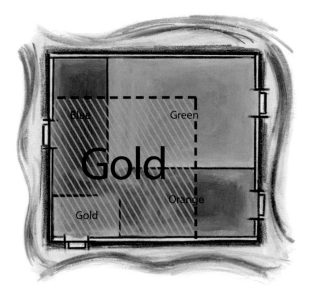

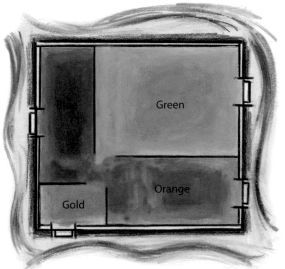

Recognizing Clean-up and Repair Needs
Figure 5.1

For better or worse, most of us adults are stuck with our Real Colors home. But you are not limited to any particular floor plan. Both of the plans in Figure 5.1 can be improved, and you now have the tools to begin your improvement project. Minor cleaning and repair is a first step in this process.

If your current Real Colors floor plan resembles the top plan in Figure 5.1, your home simply needs some clean up. You may simply need to consider the inventory questions from Chapter 3:

Inventory Questions

1) How much stuff have I collected in each room of my Real Colors home?

2) Where did my color stuff come from – parents, friends, work, personal choice, don't know?

3) How often and how effectively do I use my color stuff?

4) How comfortable do I feel when I use my color stuff?

5) How might a decision to use certain color stuff more or less affect movement throughout my Real Colors home?

The size of the rooms in your Real Colors home may not be ideal, but the flow from room to room will be enhanced by your clean-up operations. You can decide later how to move interior walls in order to balance the colors a bit more.

If your current Real Colors floor plan resembles the bottom plan in Figure 5.1, you may need to build some storage space for your Gold stuff and an exercise room to practice your preferred Green activities. You may want to create a desk within your Green room so that you have a place to work on letters and packages that you will use to return the Gold guilt that is impeding the flow of your house. Then you can take the Gold stuff you want to keep and move back into your Gold space.

You may also need to repair hinges and locks on all exterior doors since some haven't been used as much over the years. You will be surprised how much more balanced your Real Colors home will be inside and out once these doors have been repaired. Don't be afraid to ask people to use a particular door. Tell people you trust about your improvement needs. Ask for what you need. For example, you might say, "Before I can make sense of what you are telling me, I need to understand the rationale (Green) behind your request."

You can keep your Gold door open, but invite your Gold friends to spend some time in your Green room. In this case you might say, "That is a terrific goal (Gold). Let's consider for a moment the strategies (Green) we will need to follow in order to make that happen."

These clean-up and repair steps simply help you control entry into and out of your Real Colors home. They also allow you to gain better balance in terms of the flow of people and information once they enter your space.

This lays the necessary groundwork for the next three steps of your Real Colors home improvement process.

Step 2   Recalibrating Your Temperament Thermostat

Once you have cleaned and made minor repairs, it will be much easier to balance the overall climate of your Real Colors home. Your preferred color does not totally describe your temperament. Again, it is okay to be your preferred color, but you need to do all of the colors. You may describe your color order as Blue-Gold-Green-Orange, for example. But that does not mean that you can't do Orange when it is called for. The trick is in balancing your strengths and liabilities to your greatest advantage while leaving space for others to do the same. It's somewhat like trying to find a thermostat setting that works for you and the other members of your family and then realizing you need to tweak it for overnight guests.

Anyone who has shared a home with a spouse or roommate knows that tweaking a thermostat is no small feat. Figure 5.2 illustrates how you can listen for color clues using your own thermometer.

Common Questions/Comments expressing **PURPOSE**

- Why are we doing this?
- This just doesn't seem fair to people.
- If you want people to care about how much you know, let them know how much you care.

Common Questions/Comments expressing **PARAMETERS**

- Just give me the rules and get out of my way.
- That is the rule and there are no exceptions.
- Who has the authority in this matter?

Common Questions/Comments expressing **PROCESS**

- How does this work?
- Let's take a moment to look at the big picture.
- What's your plan?

Common Questions/Comments expressing **PRIORITIES**

- Let's get moving.
- Just do it.
- What are we waiting for?

Your Real Colors Thermometer
Figure 5.2

When you hear words from Figure 5.2 coming from yourself or others, they are likely to be calling for the color indicated in the thermometer. However, before you respond to such initiatives, you might want to ask yourself a few questions:

When the words are your words – *Am I hearing what I want to hear or what others are hearing?*

When they are someone else's words – *Have I interacted with this person enough to recognize the message behind the message?*

Regardless of whose words – *What else is going on here?*

Regardless of whose words – *Who else is involved in this interaction?*

Just as room conditions are not simply a result of a thermostat setting, our words are not always shaped by a temperament alone. Some people are hesitant to express themselves freely in large groups, while others find small groups or one-on-one conversations excruciating. At other times people may soften their words to make an order sound more like a request. For example, your supervisor might say, "Would you like to call 'XYZ Company' to see how we can repair our relationship with them?" In such a situation you would be ill-advised to respond, "No, thanks, Jack." You should listen for and think about the message behind the words by asking yourself the following three questions:

Have I interacted with this person enough to recognize the message behind the message?

What is going on here?

Who else is involved?

The first question is a slow down and focus question. It provides a quick-and-dirty analysis. If you know from past experience that your supervisor is Gold, you can move to your Gold response, "I'll get right on it." If you are not certain, you may want to say, "It sounds as if you're anxious to get started, Jack. Is there anything I need to know about the people at 'XYZ Company' before I call them?" This question stimulates another response so that you can listen for the message behind the words.

The second question is a purpose question. It implies a quick-and-dirty survey of the situation. If this is a party, you could respond to Jack differently than you would in a work setting. If Jack is a friend or co-worker, you might respond differently than you would to your boss. If you are responsible for this project, you may react differently than you would if you were being invited to become involved.

The third question is a group dynamics question. It implies a need to consider people's needs beyond your own Blue and Jack's Gold. If you are responsible for the event, a sales project for example, you need to determine how to adjust the temperament of this conversation. This is a situation that calls for you to adjust the thermostat setting in the room. To avoid drawing erroneous conclusions regarding appropriate responses to someone else's color initiative, you can learn to adjust your temperament thermostat. Take a look at Figure 5.3.

Temperament Thermostat
Figure 5.3

Using this figure as an example, start with the setting your temperament calls for. In this figure it is Blue. When you want to feel Blue, you will adjust your surroundings to feel Blue.

My wife and I have been happily married for almost 34 years, and we still have not agreed on a definition of "comfortable." But a recent trip to a home and garden show gave us a reason to be optimistic about finding a better way to balance our competing definitions of comfort. As we surveyed various home heating and cooling systems, we discovered the wonder of digital controls. We learned that these new systems would allow us to adjust the temperature and humidity in individual rooms, to program various settings for energy conservation, and to return automatically to our preferred settings after guests leave our home. (And we all lived happily ever after.)

Although the colors are not digitally controlled, they do allow multiple users to co-exist in close quarters. In fact, they actually encourage teamwork. Remember that this is not brain surgery. It's okay to miss the target with a question or a response. The more you practice asking the three simple questions above, the more natural, i.e., less intrusive, they will seem. The real issue is not that they are getting in the way of your success. They are simply having to compete with the questions that your brain has learned to ask automatically based on your past experiences.

When people tell me that they don't have time to second-guess everything they say, I respond, "That's absolutely correct. So don't practice in every situation." A brain surgeon seldom tries a new surgical technique in the operating room before watching others and practicing it elsewhere. But if she never tries a new technique, she may be passing up an opportunity to improve her overall skill set.

What you need to ask yourself is how important your personal interactions with others are. No one would say, "I trust my doctor even though she doesn't have any formal training. She just seems to have good surgical instincts." Yet, we seem content to trust our initial instincts when it comes to human interactions. Most of our day-to-day happiness, regardless of the setting, comes down to our ability to get along with others in a way that allows us to be ourselves. And once again you must ask yourself what is important to you, what strengths you have in any situation, what past experiences may be "coloring" your impression of a word or an action. Turn your attention now to this important area of self-discovery by examining your self-talk. Can you adjust the acoustics in your Real Colors home well enough to differentiate positive self-talk from negative self-talk?

Step 3   *Adjusting Real Colors Acoustics*

Return for a moment to the advice provided earlier in this guide. Most of your problems with gaining new temperament skills arise from your inability to appreciate your own strengths. Regardless of the point from which you are beginning your re-modeling project, you need to be certain that your

Real Colors acoustics are conducive to listening for self-talk. You don't need to be an acoustics expert to improve the noise levels in your environment. If parents, family, or work associates have prevented you from hearing positive feedback about your color order, you may simply need to turn down their speakers and turn up the volume on your own self-talk. But be certain first that your own radio channel is playing positive messages. Take a moment to review what makes you effective.

Self-talk is not about struggling with voices. That is a medical problem. But most of us hear recordings of voices from our past that play somewhat as follows:

Reinforcing voices
That was tremendous.
You are incredible.
I never saw someone do that before.
What a good little boy/girl you are.
Always remember to. . .

Reprimanding or righteous indignation voices
Why can't you follow directions?
You aren't listening to me.
You are the most self-centered person I have ever met.
What a klutz you are.

What is the self-talk that goes on in your head every day? You have to listen closely because sometimes we tune them out – either because they are too painful or because they seem to be givens. Here are some tips for reflecting on self-talk.

If your self-talk has discouraged you from collecting your own color stuff...
Your recordings are negative.
Your recordings cause you to feel guilty.
Your recordings confirm your ineptitude.

If your self-talk has encouraged you to collect too much of your own color stuff...
Your recordings are positive.
Your recordings cause you to feel a sense of pride in the way you do things.
Your recordings confirm your ability to tackle new problems.

Sometimes a little guilt is a good thing. After all, we aren't perfect. However, we don't gain a positive attitude and a sense of resiliency from a constant diet of negativity. Success feeds success. Again, flow emerges from receiving feedback from experiences that confirm what we are doing is achieving the results we want. Ask yourself what your parents rewarded or discouraged during your childhood and adolescence. How positive was your school experience and from what source did you receive the most positive or negative feedback – academics, sports, music performance, etc.? To what extent does your work experience provide you with positive feedback? What do you like about what you do?

Reflecting on self-talk requires that you pay attention to what is happening during those moments when you feel "up" as well as what is happening during those moments when you feel "down." As difficult as it might seem, you can learn to take stock of yourself at these key moments. Carry a notebook that fits into your pocket. Or learn to keep a daily "Ups and Downs" journal. Then go back weekly and eventually monthly to look for patterns in these notes. The patterns will emerge slowly. After all, patterns require multiple experiences. But once you spot them, they are often so pronounced that you will wonder how you had missed them for so long.

Figure 5.4 addresses the question: "When is enough insufficient, enough, or too much?" It illustrates the point that "one person's trash could be another person's treasure."

Color	Insufficient	Enough	Too Much
All Colors	Feeling unappreciated and misunderstood	Feeling successful, appreciated, and at one with the world	Feeling a need to protect what you have from others

Trash or Treasure?
Figure 5.4

⟲ Real Colors Home Improvement

There is no absolute when it comes to determining whether you have too little, too much, or just the right amount of your color. However, Figure 5.4 illustrates that the feelings that accompany these emotions are common among all the colors. When we are not given adequate positive feedback regarding our temperament, we typically feel unappreciated and misunderstood. Most of us do what we do with good intentions. And while we tend to judge others based on their behavior, we want others to judge us according to our intentions — or at least to factor in those intentions.

When you receive adequate positive feedback for your words and actions, you feel successful, appreciated, and at one with the world. At these times you will work beyond anyone's expectations, even your own, for the sheer joy of the experience. At these times life assumes an incredible three-way balance among your intentions, the expectations of others, and the results.

Once you get a taste for positive feedback, you may not be able to get enough. You may crave opportunities to experience it. Eventually you may even start to compare how much of it you have as compared to someone else. Soon you are competing with others and protecting what you have so that others can't steal it from you. At its worst, this state goes to a point at which you might consider stealing a bit from others to add to your own treasures. You become so self-absorbed that you develop a need to be the center of attention at all times. Let's take a moment to consider how these three states emerge differently from one color to another. What does too little or too much look like for a Blue, Green, Gold, or Orange?

Too little...

Blue – pouting, withdrawal, self-pity
Green – sarcastic, erratic, and argumentative behavior
Gold – angry, questioning the dedication and commitment of others, searching
    for the rulebook
Orange – restless, belligerent, drawing the line in the sand

Too much...

Blue – wide-eyed and prone to trust others without questioning
Green – self-absorbed and prone to pontificate
Gold – self-righteous and prone to see the world in absolutes
Orange – excited and prone to overwhelm others with banter and activity

As you reflect on your self-talk and how others perceive you, look beyond the obvious. If the thermostat in your Real Colors environment seems out of sync, you might want to ask yourself if you're sitting in a draft of your own making. If so, perhaps you need a sweater. Or is your area of the room simply too hot due to too much of another color emanating from the people around you. If so, you might want to move to another spot. And finally, if there is no hope of finding a comfortable spot in this environment, you might consider avoiding these people or this situation in the future. Remember that you aren't always in control of the thermostat. And when you are, you may want to tweak it so you don't drive everyone else away.

Step 4   Conducting an Open House

One of the most difficult tasks I faced in my days as a middle school principal was helping young people reintroduce themselves to their teachers, parents, and friends following a string of discipline problems. A child of 11-14 years of age has developed both habits and an image. For me the first challenge in dealing with discipline issues in emerging adolescents was always to get them to admit their responsibilities for a problem. Otherwise, they could place the blame squarely on others – a characteristic that is also present in most criminals. When you ask middle schoolers why they are in the principal's office, repeat offenders will typically begin their responses with, "The teacher…" At that point a savvy principal responds, "No, I didn't ask what the teacher did. I asked what you did to get here. Or are you telling me that Mr. Smith lies awake at night thinking of ways to get you?"

After several minutes of these exchanges, the focus moves to changing the child's behavior. But the conference is incomplete unless the principal gives the repentant child some advice on reintroducing himself to the world.

Having dried tears and strutted out the office door, any self-respecting middle schooler must retain an air of confidence. When asked by inquiring classmates what happened, he must respond with a grin, "Nothing; just the same boring stuff." This response is plausible to most of his classmates and helps the rehabilitated student save face. Unfortunately, the answer is often equally plausible to teachers passing by who storm to the office demanding justice or who hone their antennae to catch this unremorseful student the next time he makes a misstep.

Although this scene may play out differently in the adult world, the general nature of events usually emerges along similar lines. For numerous reasons already mentioned, it is often difficult for an individual to change fundamental attitudes and behaviors. And the final stumbling block to assuming a new you is often found in the preconceptions of friends, family, and acquaintances. Therefore, there are some simple guidelines that can help you deal with these obstacles.

Don't assume that a minor Real Colors remodeling effort can always be accomplished without the support of friends and acquaintances.

Don't assume that every person wants you to fail in your transformation.

Don't be afraid to tell close friends and family what you are trying to accomplish in terms of your Real Colors remodeling effort.

Do express optimism without sounding too self-assured.

Do describe the type of feedback you need, or you may not get it.

Do take the risk to change, but take it in small, manageable steps.

Habits take a long time to develop. Often they take much longer to change. While people may want to help you during your remodeling efforts, don't forget that they may be deeply involved in their own remodeling projects. It is very important that you maintain the existing portions of your Real Colors home and keep the premises clean enough that you still feel comfortable entertaining friends. Don't lose sight of who you are. Follow the patterns from your "Ups and Downs" journal. Most likely you will see the pattern of a dynamic person, knowledgeable and capable of interacting effectively with others.

And as a footnote to parents – don't forget that it is much simpler and less expensive to build a new home than to remodel an existing structure, especially one that has fallen into disrepair. As you watch your children grow, look for color clues in their words and actions. Remember that you are serving as a daily role model for them as they build their own Real Colors home. Take the time to find out what rooms they enjoy most. Be supportive of their tastes without overindulging them. Protect them from overzealous neighbors, friends, and teachers without shielding them from other Real Colors floor plans. In the end, your Real Colors legacy will be determined by your ability to model balance rather than defining or demanding it.

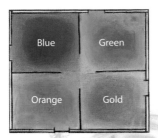

1. Take a look at your Real Colors floor plan. Are any of your internal doors cluttered or your external doors closed off? Which ones, and how will you clean-up and perform minor repairs? _____

_____

_____

2. Circle the Real Colors thermostat setting that you prefer. Then underline the one that provides the least comfort (first and last color respectively in your color order).

3. Indicate whether you have too little, too much, or just enough of each of your first color.

Your First Color _____

Insufficient	Enough	Too Much
☐	☐	☐
Feeling unappreciated and misunderstood	Feeling successful, appreciated, and at one with the world	Feeling a need to protect what you have from others

4. Given your answer to number 3, will you begin your remodeling effort by adding or pitching color "stuff?" If you need help with this project, where will you find it?

_____

_____

5. What specific parameters will you set for feedback on your remodeling project?

_____

_____

6. Using a pocket-sized notepad, create an "Ups and Downs" journal. Keep the journal for a month or so before answering the next several questions. Be certain to jot down where you are, the people present, and what you are doing when you feel particularly positive or negative.

7. What is a realistic timetable for various phases of this remodeling project?

Dreaming _____

Designing _____

Doing_____

8. What obstacles and support do you anticipate needing as you reintroduce yourself to the world?

   Obstacles _____

   Support _____

9. What opportunities do you have to assist others in remodeling their Real
   Colors homes? _____

   _____

   _____

   _____

   _____

10. What opportunities do you have to assist others in building their Real
    Colors homes – your children, nieces and nephews, grandchildren,
    students, or children in your community? _____

    _____

    _____

    _____

    _____

◎ Bibliography

Csikszentmihalyi, M. *Flow*. New York: Harper & Row, 1990.

Covey, S. *The Seven Habits of Highly Effective People: Restoring the Character Ethic*. New York: Simon and Schuster, 1989.

Keirsey, D. & Bates, M. *Please Understand Me II: Temperament, Character, Intelligence*. Del Mar, CA: Prometheus Memesis Books, 1998.

Johnson, D. *Balanced Leadership for REAL Change*. Manuscript in progress, 2003.

Myers, I. Manual: *The Myers-Briggs Type Indicator*. Palo Alto, CA: Consulting Psychologists Press, 1962.